To:

_____

From:

_____

Date:

_____

DELIGHT YOURSELF IN THE LORD,
AND HE WILL GIVE YOU THE DESIRES OF YOUR HEART.

PSALM 37:4

THE LORD IS MY LIGHT AND MY SALVATION—
WHOM SHALL I FEAR? THE LORD IS THE STRONGHOLD OF
MY LIFE—OF WHOM SHALL I BE AFRAID? PSALM 27:1

THE LORD HIMSELF GOES BEFORE YOU AND WILL BE WITH YOU;
HE WILL NEVER LEAVE YOU NOR FORSAKE YOU.

DEUTERONOMY 31:8

GOD IS WORKING IN YOU, GIVING YOU THE DESIRE
TO OBEY HIM AND THE POWER TO DO WHAT PLEASES HIM.

PHILIPPIANS 2:13

I CAN DO EVERYTHING THROUGH CHRIST, WHO GIVES ME STRENGTH.

PHILIPPIANS 4:13

IF YOU WANT TO KNOW WHAT GOD WANTS YOU TO DO,
ASK HIM, AND HE WILL GLADLY TELL YOU.

JAMES 1:5

CREATE IN ME A PURE HEART, O GOD,
AND RENEW A STEADFAST SPIRIT WITHIN ME.

PSALM 51:10

IF ANYONE IS IN CHRIST, HE IS A NEW CREATION;
THE OLD HAS GONE, THE NEW HAS COME!

2 CORINTHIANS 5:17

CAST YOUR CARES ON THE LORD AND HE WILL SUSTAIN YOU.

PSALM 55:22

THE LORD YOUR GOD IS WITH YOU, HE IS MIGHTY TO SAVE.
HE WILL TAKE GREAT DELIGHT IN YOU, HE WILL QUIET YOU
WITH HIS LOVE. ZEPHANIAH 3:17

THE LORD IS FAITHFUL TO ALL HIS PROMISES
AND LOVING TOWARD ALL HE HAS MADE.

PSALM 145:13

IN YOU, O LORD, DO I PUT MY TRUST AND CONFIDENTLY
TAKE REFUGE; LET ME NEVER BE PUT TO SHAME OR CONFUSION!

PSALM 71:1

"BE STRONG AND COURAGEOUS . . . THE LORD YOUR GOD
WILL BE WITH YOU WHEREVER YOU GO."

JOSHUA 1:9

DEPEND ON THE LORD IN WHATEVER YOU DO,
AND YOUR PLANS WILL SUCCEED.

PROVERBS 16:3

SINCE WE HAVE BEEN JUSTIFIED THROUGH FAITH,
WE HAVE PEACE WITH GOD THROUGH OUR LORD JESUS CHRIST.

ROMANS 5:1

THE LORD IS MY ROCK, MY FORTRESS AND MY DELIVERER;
MY GOD IS MY ROCK, IN WHOM I TAKE REFUGE.

PSALM 18:2

"IF ANYONE WOULD COME AFTER ME, HE MUST DENY HIMSELF
AND TAKE UP HIS CROSS AND FOLLOW ME."

MATTHEW 16:24

THE WORD OF THE LORD IS RIGHT AND TRUE;
HE IS FAITHFUL IN ALL HE DOES.

PSALM 33:4

THE LORD IS MY STRENGTH, MY SHIELD FROM EVERY DANGER.
I TRUST IN HIM WITH ALL MY HEART.

PSALM 28:7

IN HIM WE HAVE REDEMPTION THROUGH HIS BLOOD,
THE FORGIVENESS OF SINS, IN ACCORDANCE
WITH THE RICHES OF GOD'S GRACE. EPHESIANS 1:7

I TRUST IN YOUR UNFAILING LOVE. I WILL REJOICE BECAUSE
YOU HAVE RESCUED ME. I WILL SING TO THE LORD BECAUSE
HE HAS BEEN SO GOOD TO ME. PSALM 13:5-6

LIVE A LIFE OF LOVE, JUST AS CHRIST LOVED US AND
GAVE HIMSELF UP FOR US AS A FRAGRANT OFFERING
AND SACRIFICE TO GOD. EPHESIANS 5:2

"YOU WILL CALL UPON ME AND COME AND PRAY TO ME, AND I WILL
LISTEN TO YOU. YOU WILL SEEK ME AND FIND ME WHEN YOU SEEK ME
WITH ALL YOUR HEART." JEREMIAH 29:12-13

MY SOUL FINDS REST IN GOD ALONE; MY SALVATION COMES FROM HIM.

PSALM 62:1

DELIGHT YOURSELF IN THE LORD,
AND HE WILL GIVE YOU THE DESIRES OF YOUR HEART.

PSALM 37:4

THE LORD IS MY LIGHT AND MY SALVATION—
WHOM SHALL I FEAR? THE LORD IS THE STRONGHOLD OF
MY LIFE—OF WHOM SHALL I BE AFRAID? PSALM 27:1

THE LORD HIMSELF GOES BEFORE YOU AND WILL BE WITH YOU;
HE WILL NEVER LEAVE YOU NOR FORSAKE YOU.

DEUTERONOMY 31:8

GOD IS WORKING IN YOU, GIVING YOU THE DESIRE
TO OBEY HIM AND THE POWER TO DO WHAT PLEASES HIM.

PHILIPPIANS 2:13

I CAN DO EVERYTHING THROUGH CHRIST, WHO GIVES ME STRENGTH.

PHILIPPIANS 4:13

IF YOU WANT TO KNOW WHAT GOD WANTS YOU TO DO,
ASK HIM, AND HE WILL GLADLY TELL YOU.

JAMES 1:5

CREATE IN ME A PURE HEART, O GOD,
AND RENEW A STEADFAST SPIRIT WITHIN ME.

PSALM 51:10

IF ANYONE IS IN CHRIST, HE IS A NEW CREATION;
THE OLD HAS GONE, THE NEW HAS COME!

2 CORINTHIANS 5:17

CAST YOUR CARES ON THE LORD AND HE WILL SUSTAIN YOU.

PSALM 55:22

THE LORD YOUR GOD IS WITH YOU, HE IS MIGHTY TO SAVE.
HE WILL TAKE GREAT DELIGHT IN YOU, HE WILL QUIET YOU
WITH HIS LOVE. ZEPHANIAH 3:17

THE LORD IS FAITHFUL TO ALL HIS PROMISES
AND LOVING TOWARD ALL HE HAS MADE.

PSALM 145:13

IN YOU, O LORD, DO I PUT MY TRUST AND CONFIDENTLY
TAKE REFUGE; LET ME NEVER BE PUT TO SHAME OR CONFUSION!

PSALM 71:1

"BE STRONG AND COURAGEOUS . . . THE LORD YOUR GOD
WILL BE WITH YOU WHEREVER YOU GO."

JOSHUA 1:9

DEPEND ON THE LORD IN WHATEVER YOU DO,
AND YOUR PLANS WILL SUCCEED.

PROVERBS 16:3

SINCE WE HAVE BEEN JUSTIFIED THROUGH FAITH,
WE HAVE PEACE WITH GOD THROUGH OUR LORD JESUS CHRIST.

ROMANS 5:1

THE LORD IS MY ROCK, MY FORTRESS AND MY DELIVERER;
MY GOD IS MY ROCK, IN WHOM I TAKE REFUGE.

PSALM 18:2

"IF ANYONE WOULD COME AFTER ME, HE MUST DENY HIMSELF
AND TAKE UP HIS CROSS AND FOLLOW ME."

MATTHEW 16:24

THE WORD OF THE LORD IS RIGHT AND TRUE;
HE IS FAITHFUL IN ALL HE DOES.

PSALM 33:4

THE LORD IS MY STRENGTH, MY SHIELD FROM EVERY DANGER.
I TRUST IN HIM WITH ALL MY HEART.

PSALM 28:7

IN HIM WE HAVE REDEMPTION THROUGH HIS BLOOD,
THE FORGIVENESS OF SINS, IN ACCORDANCE
WITH THE RICHES OF GOD'S GRACE. EPHESIANS 1:7

I TRUST IN YOUR UNFAILING LOVE. I WILL REJOICE BECAUSE
YOU HAVE RESCUED ME. I WILL SING TO THE LORD BECAUSE
HE HAS BEEN SO GOOD TO ME.   PSALM 13:5-6

LIVE A LIFE OF LOVE, JUST AS CHRIST LOVED US AND
GAVE HIMSELF UP FOR US AS A FRAGRANT OFFERING
AND SACRIFICE TO GOD. EPHESIANS 5:2

"YOU WILL CALL UPON ME AND COME AND PRAY TO ME, AND I WILL
LISTEN TO YOU. YOU WILL SEEK ME AND FIND ME WHEN YOU SEEK ME
WITH ALL YOUR HEART." JEREMIAH 29:12-13

MY SOUL FINDS REST IN GOD ALONE; MY SALVATION COMES FROM HIM.

DELIGHT YOURSELF IN THE LORD,
AND HE WILL GIVE YOU THE DESIRES OF YOUR HEART.

PSALM 37:4

THE LORD IS MY LIGHT AND MY SALVATION—
WHOM SHALL I FEAR? THE LORD IS THE STRONGHOLD OF
MY LIFE—OF WHOM SHALL I BE AFRAID? PSALM 27:1

THE LORD HIMSELF GOES BEFORE YOU AND WILL BE WITH YOU;
HE WILL NEVER LEAVE YOU NOR FORSAKE YOU.

DEUTERONOMY 31:8

GOD IS WORKING IN YOU, GIVING YOU THE DESIRE
TO OBEY HIM AND THE POWER TO DO WHAT PLEASES HIM.

PHILIPPIANS 2:13

I CAN DO EVERYTHING THROUGH CHRIST, WHO GIVES ME STRENGTH.

PHILIPPIANS 4:13

IF YOU WANT TO KNOW WHAT GOD WANTS YOU TO DO,
ASK HIM, AND HE WILL GLADLY TELL YOU.

JAMES 1:5

CREATE IN ME A PURE HEART, O GOD,
AND RENEW A STEADFAST SPIRIT WITHIN ME.

PSALM 51:10

IF ANYONE IS IN CHRIST, HE IS A NEW CREATION;
THE OLD HAS GONE, THE NEW HAS COME!

2 CORINTHIANS 5:17

CAST YOUR CARES ON THE LORD AND HE WILL SUSTAIN YOU.

PSALM 55:22

THE LORD YOUR GOD IS WITH YOU, HE IS MIGHTY TO SAVE.
HE WILL TAKE GREAT DELIGHT IN YOU, HE WILL QUIET YOU
WITH HIS LOVE. ZEPHANIAH 3:17

THE LORD IS FAITHFUL TO ALL HIS PROMISES
AND LOVING TOWARD ALL HE HAS MADE.

PSALM 145:13

IN YOU, O LORD, DO I PUT MY TRUST AND CONFIDENTLY
TAKE REFUGE; LET ME NEVER BE PUT TO SHAME OR CONFUSION!

PSALM 71:1

"BE STRONG AND COURAGEOUS . . . THE LORD YOUR GOD
WILL BE WITH YOU WHEREVER YOU GO."

JOSHUA 1:9

DEPEND ON THE LORD IN WHATEVER YOU DO,
AND YOUR PLANS WILL SUCCEED.

PROVERBS 16:3

SINCE WE HAVE BEEN JUSTIFIED THROUGH FAITH,
WE HAVE PEACE WITH GOD THROUGH OUR LORD JESUS CHRIST.

ROMANS 5:1

THE LORD IS MY ROCK, MY FORTRESS AND MY DELIVERER;
MY GOD IS MY ROCK, IN WHOM I TAKE REFUGE.

PSALM 18:2

"IF ANYONE WOULD COME AFTER ME, HE MUST DENY HIMSELF
AND TAKE UP HIS CROSS AND FOLLOW ME."

MATTHEW 16:24

THE WORD OF THE LORD IS RIGHT AND TRUE;
HE IS FAITHFUL IN ALL HE DOES.

PSALM 33:4

THE LORD IS MY STRENGTH, MY SHIELD FROM EVERY DANGER.
I TRUST IN HIM WITH ALL MY HEART.

PSALM 28:7

IN HIM WE HAVE REDEMPTION THROUGH HIS BLOOD,
THE FORGIVENESS OF SINS, IN ACCORDANCE
WITH THE RICHES OF GOD'S GRACE. EPHESIANS 1:7

I TRUST IN YOUR UNFAILING LOVE. I WILL REJOICE BECAUSE
YOU HAVE RESCUED ME. I WILL SING TO THE LORD BECAUSE
HE HAS BEEN SO GOOD TO ME. PSALM 13:5-6

LIVE A LIFE OF LOVE, JUST AS CHRIST LOVED US AND
GAVE HIMSELF UP FOR US AS A FRAGRANT OFFERING
AND SACRIFICE TO GOD. EPHESIANS 5:2

"YOU WILL CALL UPON ME AND COME AND PRAY TO ME, AND I WILL
LISTEN TO YOU. YOU WILL SEEK ME AND FIND ME WHEN YOU SEEK ME
WITH ALL YOUR HEART." JEREMIAH 29:12-13

MY SOUL FINDS REST IN GOD ALONE; MY SALVATION COMES FROM HIM.

PSALM 62:1

DELIGHT YOURSELF IN THE LORD,
AND HE WILL GIVE YOU THE DESIRES OF YOUR HEART.

PSALM 37:4

THE LORD IS MY LIGHT AND MY SALVATION—
WHOM SHALL I FEAR? THE LORD IS THE STRONGHOLD OF
MY LIFE—OF WHOM SHALL I BE AFRAID? PSALM 27:1

THE LORD HIMSELF GOES BEFORE YOU AND WILL BE WITH YOU;
HE WILL NEVER LEAVE YOU NOR FORSAKE YOU.

DEUTERONOMY 31:8

GOD IS WORKING IN YOU, GIVING YOU THE DESIRE
TO OBEY HIM AND THE POWER TO DO WHAT PLEASES HIM.

PHILIPPIANS 2:13

I CAN DO EVERYTHING THROUGH CHRIST, WHO GIVES ME STRENGTH.

PHILIPPIANS 4:13

IF YOU WANT TO KNOW WHAT GOD WANTS YOU TO DO,
ASK HIM, AND HE WILL GLADLY TELL YOU.

JAMES 1:5

CREATE IN ME A PURE HEART, O GOD,
AND RENEW A STEADFAST SPIRIT WITHIN ME.

PSALM 51:10

IF ANYONE IS IN CHRIST, HE IS A NEW CREATION;
THE OLD HAS GONE, THE NEW HAS COME!

2 CORINTHIANS 5:17

CAST YOUR CARES ON THE LORD AND HE WILL SUSTAIN YOU.

PSALM 55:22

THE LORD YOUR GOD IS WITH YOU, HE IS MIGHTY TO SAVE.
HE WILL TAKE GREAT DELIGHT IN YOU, HE WILL QUIET YOU
WITH HIS LOVE. ZEPHANIAH 3:17

THE LORD IS FAITHFUL TO ALL HIS PROMISES
AND LOVING TOWARD ALL HE HAS MADE.

PSALM 145:13

IN YOU, O LORD, DO I PUT MY TRUST AND CONFIDENTLY
TAKE REFUGE; LET ME NEVER BE PUT TO SHAME OR CONFUSION!

PSALM 71:1

"BE STRONG AND COURAGEOUS . . . THE LORD YOUR GOD
WILL BE WITH YOU WHEREVER YOU GO."

JOSHUA 1:9

DEPEND ON THE LORD IN WHATEVER YOU DO,
AND YOUR PLANS WILL SUCCEED.

PROVERBS 16:3

SINCE WE HAVE BEEN JUSTIFIED THROUGH FAITH,
WE HAVE PEACE WITH GOD THROUGH OUR LORD JESUS CHRIST.

ROMANS 5:1

THE LORD IS MY ROCK, MY FORTRESS AND MY DELIVERER;
MY GOD IS MY ROCK, IN WHOM I TAKE REFUGE.

PSALM 18:2

"IF ANYONE WOULD COME AFTER ME, HE MUST DENY HIMSELF
AND TAKE UP HIS CROSS AND FOLLOW ME."

MATTHEW 16:24

THE WORD OF THE LORD IS RIGHT AND TRUE;
HE IS FAITHFUL IN ALL HE DOES.

PSALM 33:4

THE LORD IS MY STRENGTH, MY SHIELD FROM EVERY DANGER.
I TRUST IN HIM WITH ALL MY HEART.

PSALM 28:7

IN HIM WE HAVE REDEMPTION THROUGH HIS BLOOD,
THE FORGIVENESS OF SINS, IN ACCORDANCE
WITH THE RICHES OF GOD'S GRACE. EPHESIANS 1:7

I TRUST IN YOUR UNFAILING LOVE. I WILL REJOICE BECAUSE
YOU HAVE RESCUED ME. I WILL SING TO THE LORD BECAUSE
HE HAS BEEN SO GOOD TO ME. PSALM 13:5-6

LIVE A LIFE OF LOVE, JUST AS CHRIST LOVED US AND
GAVE HIMSELF UP FOR US AS A FRAGRANT OFFERING
AND SACRIFICE TO GOD. EPHESIANS 5:2

"YOU WILL CALL UPON ME AND COME AND PRAY TO ME, AND I WILL
LISTEN TO YOU. YOU WILL SEEK ME AND FIND ME WHEN YOU SEEK ME
WITH ALL YOUR HEART." JEREMIAH 29:12-13

MY SOUL FINDS REST IN GOD ALONE; MY SALVATION COMES FROM HIM.

PSALM 62:1

DELIGHT YOURSELF IN THE LORD,
AND HE WILL GIVE YOU THE DESIRES OF YOUR HEART.

PSALM 37:4

THE LORD IS MY LIGHT AND MY SALVATION—
WHOM SHALL I FEAR? THE LORD IS THE STRONGHOLD OF
MY LIFE—OF WHOM SHALL I BE AFRAID? PSALM 27:1

THE LORD HIMSELF GOES BEFORE YOU AND WILL BE WITH YOU;
HE WILL NEVER LEAVE YOU NOR FORSAKE YOU.

DEUTERONOMY 31:8

GOD IS WORKING IN YOU, GIVING YOU THE DESIRE
TO OBEY HIM AND THE POWER TO DO WHAT PLEASES HIM.

PHILIPPIANS 2:13

I CAN DO EVERYTHING THROUGH CHRIST, WHO GIVES ME STRENGTH.

PHILIPPIANS 4:13

IF YOU WANT TO KNOW WHAT GOD WANTS YOU TO DO,
ASK HIM, AND HE WILL GLADLY TELL YOU.

JAMES 1:5

CREATE IN ME A PURE HEART, O GOD,
AND RENEW A STEADFAST SPIRIT WITHIN ME.

PSALM 51:10

IF ANYONE IS IN CHRIST, HE IS A NEW CREATION;
THE OLD HAS GONE, THE NEW HAS COME!

2 CORINTHIANS 5:17

CAST YOUR CARES ON THE LORD AND HE WILL SUSTAIN YOU.

PSALM 55:22

THE LORD YOUR GOD IS WITH YOU, HE IS MIGHTY TO SAVE.
HE WILL TAKE GREAT DELIGHT IN YOU, HE WILL QUIET YOU
WITH HIS LOVE. ZEPHANIAH 3:17

THE LORD IS FAITHFUL TO ALL HIS PROMISES
AND LOVING TOWARD ALL HE HAS MADE.

PSALM 145:13

IN YOU, O LORD, DO I PUT MY TRUST AND CONFIDENTLY
TAKE REFUGE; LET ME NEVER BE PUT TO SHAME OR CONFUSION!

PSALM 71:1

"BE STRONG AND COURAGEOUS . . . THE LORD YOUR GOD
WILL BE WITH YOU WHEREVER YOU GO."

JOSHUA 1:9

DEPEND ON THE LORD IN WHATEVER YOU DO,
AND YOUR PLANS WILL SUCCEED.

PROVERBS 16:3

SINCE WE HAVE BEEN JUSTIFIED THROUGH FAITH,
WE HAVE PEACE WITH GOD THROUGH OUR LORD JESUS CHRIST.

ROMANS 5:1

THE LORD IS MY ROCK, MY FORTRESS AND MY DELIVERER;
MY GOD IS MY ROCK, IN WHOM I TAKE REFUGE.

PSALM 18:2

"IF ANYONE WOULD COME AFTER ME, HE MUST DENY HIMSELF
AND TAKE UP HIS CROSS AND FOLLOW ME."

MATTHEW 16:24

THE WORD OF THE LORD IS RIGHT AND TRUE;
HE IS FAITHFUL IN ALL HE DOES.

PSALM 33:4

THE LORD IS MY STRENGTH, MY SHIELD FROM EVERY DANGER.
I TRUST IN HIM WITH ALL MY HEART.

PSALM 28:7

IN HIM WE HAVE REDEMPTION THROUGH HIS BLOOD,
THE FORGIVENESS OF SINS, IN ACCORDANCE
WITH THE RICHES OF GOD'S GRACE. EPHESIANS 1:7

I TRUST IN YOUR UNFAILING LOVE. I WILL REJOICE BECAUSE
YOU HAVE RESCUED ME. I WILL SING TO THE LORD BECAUSE
HE HAS BEEN SO GOOD TO ME. PSALM 13:5-6

LIVE A LIFE OF LOVE, JUST AS CHRIST LOVED US AND
GAVE HIMSELF UP FOR US AS A FRAGRANT OFFERING
AND SACRIFICE TO GOD. EPHESIANS 5:2

"YOU WILL CALL UPON ME AND COME AND PRAY TO ME, AND I WILL LISTEN TO YOU. YOU WILL SEEK ME AND FIND ME WHEN YOU SEEK ME WITH ALL YOUR HEART." JEREMIAH 29:12-13

MY SOUL FINDS REST IN GOD ALONE; MY SALVATION COMES FROM HIM.

PSALM 62:1

DELIGHT YOURSELF IN THE LORD,
AND HE WILL GIVE YOU THE DESIRES OF YOUR HEART.

PSALM 37:4

THE LORD IS MY LIGHT AND MY SALVATION—
WHOM SHALL I FEAR? THE LORD IS THE STRONGHOLD OF
MY LIFE—OF WHOM SHALL I BE AFRAID? PSALM 27:1

THE LORD HIMSELF GOES BEFORE YOU AND WILL BE WITH YOU;
HE WILL NEVER LEAVE YOU NOR FORSAKE YOU.

DEUTERONOMY 31:8

GOD IS WORKING IN YOU, GIVING YOU THE DESIRE
TO OBEY HIM AND THE POWER TO DO WHAT PLEASES HIM.

PHILIPPIANS 2:13

I CAN DO EVERYTHING THROUGH CHRIST, WHO GIVES ME STRENGTH.

PHILIPPIANS 4:13

IF YOU WANT TO KNOW WHAT GOD WANTS YOU TO DO,
ASK HIM, AND HE WILL GLADLY TELL YOU.

JAMES 1:5

CREATE IN ME A PURE HEART, O GOD,
AND RENEW A STEADFAST SPIRIT WITHIN ME.

PSALM 51:10

IF ANYONE IS IN CHRIST, HE IS A NEW CREATION;
THE OLD HAS GONE, THE NEW HAS COME!

2 CORINTHIANS 5:17

CAST YOUR CARES ON THE LORD AND HE WILL SUSTAIN YOU.

PSALM 55:22

THE LORD YOUR GOD IS WITH YOU, HE IS MIGHTY TO SAVE.
HE WILL TAKE GREAT DELIGHT IN YOU, HE WILL QUIET YOU
WITH HIS LOVE. ZEPHANIAH 3:17

THE LORD IS FAITHFUL TO ALL HIS PROMISES
AND LOVING TOWARD ALL HE HAS MADE.

PSALM 145:13

IN YOU, O LORD, DO I PUT MY TRUST AND CONFIDENTLY
TAKE REFUGE; LET ME NEVER BE PUT TO SHAME OR CONFUSION!

PSALM 71:1

"BE STRONG AND COURAGEOUS . . . THE LORD YOUR GOD
WILL BE WITH YOU WHEREVER YOU GO."

JOSHUA 1:9

DEPEND ON THE LORD IN WHATEVER YOU DO,
AND YOUR PLANS WILL SUCCEED.

PROVERBS 16:3

SINCE WE HAVE BEEN JUSTIFIED THROUGH FAITH,
WE HAVE PEACE WITH GOD THROUGH OUR LORD JESUS CHRIST.

ROMANS 5:1

THE LORD IS MY ROCK, MY FORTRESS AND MY DELIVERER;
MY GOD IS MY ROCK, IN WHOM I TAKE REFUGE.

PSALM 18:2

"IF ANYONE WOULD COME AFTER ME, HE MUST DENY HIMSELF
AND TAKE UP HIS CROSS AND FOLLOW ME."

MATTHEW 16:24

THE WORD OF THE LORD IS RIGHT AND TRUE;
HE IS FAITHFUL IN ALL HE DOES.

PSALM 33:4

THE LORD IS MY STRENGTH, MY SHIELD FROM EVERY DANGER.
I TRUST IN HIM WITH ALL MY HEART.

PSALM 28:7

IN HIM WE HAVE REDEMPTION THROUGH HIS BLOOD,
THE FORGIVENESS OF SINS, IN ACCORDANCE
WITH THE RICHES OF GOD'S GRACE. EPHESIANS 1:7

I TRUST IN YOUR UNFAILING LOVE. I WILL REJOICE BECAUSE
YOU HAVE RESCUED ME. I WILL SING TO THE LORD BECAUSE
HE HAS BEEN SO GOOD TO ME.   PSALM 13:5-6

LIVE A LIFE OF LOVE, JUST AS CHRIST LOVED US AND
GAVE HIMSELF UP FOR US AS A FRAGRANT OFFERING
AND SACRIFICE TO GOD. EPHESIANS 5:2

"YOU WILL CALL UPON ME AND COME AND PRAY TO ME, AND I WILL
LISTEN TO YOU. YOU WILL SEEK ME AND FIND ME WHEN YOU SEEK ME
WITH ALL YOUR HEART." JEREMIAH 29:12-13

MY SOUL FINDS REST IN GOD ALONE; MY SALVATION COMES FROM HIM.

PSALM 62:1

DELIGHT YOURSELF IN THE LORD,
AND HE WILL GIVE YOU THE DESIRES OF YOUR HEART.

PSALM 37:4

THE LORD IS MY LIGHT AND MY SALVATION—
WHOM SHALL I FEAR? THE LORD IS THE STRONGHOLD OF
MY LIFE—OF WHOM SHALL I BE AFRAID? PSALM 27:1

THE LORD HIMSELF GOES BEFORE YOU AND WILL BE WITH YOU;
HE WILL NEVER LEAVE YOU NOR FORSAKE YOU.

DEUTERONOMY 31:8

GOD IS WORKING IN YOU, GIVING YOU THE DESIRE
TO OBEY HIM AND THE POWER TO DO WHAT PLEASES HIM.

PHILIPPIANS 2:13

I CAN DO EVERYTHING THROUGH CHRIST, WHO GIVES ME STRENGTH.

PHILIPPIANS 4:13

IF YOU WANT TO KNOW WHAT GOD WANTS YOU TO DO,
ASK HIM, AND HE WILL GLADLY TELL YOU.

JAMES 1:5

CREATE IN ME A PURE HEART, O GOD,
AND RENEW A STEADFAST SPIRIT WITHIN ME.

PSALM 51:10

IF ANYONE IS IN CHRIST, HE IS A NEW CREATION;
THE OLD HAS GONE, THE NEW HAS COME!

2 CORINTHIANS 5:17

CAST YOUR CARES ON THE LORD AND HE WILL SUSTAIN YOU.

PSALM 55:22

THE LORD YOUR GOD IS WITH YOU, HE IS MIGHTY TO SAVE.
HE WILL TAKE GREAT DELIGHT IN YOU, HE WILL QUIET YOU
WITH HIS LOVE. ZEPHANIAH 3:17

THE LORD IS FAITHFUL TO ALL HIS PROMISES
AND LOVING TOWARD ALL HE HAS MADE.

PSALM 145:13

IN YOU, O LORD, DO I PUT MY TRUST AND CONFIDENTLY
TAKE REFUGE; LET ME NEVER BE PUT TO SHAME OR CONFUSION!

PSALM 71:1

"BE STRONG AND COURAGEOUS . . . THE LORD YOUR GOD
WILL BE WITH YOU WHEREVER YOU GO."

JOSHUA 1:9

DEPEND ON THE LORD IN WHATEVER YOU DO,
AND YOUR PLANS WILL SUCCEED.

PROVERBS 16:3

SINCE WE HAVE BEEN JUSTIFIED THROUGH FAITH,
WE HAVE PEACE WITH GOD THROUGH OUR LORD JESUS CHRIST.

ROMANS 5:1

THE LORD IS MY ROCK, MY FORTRESS AND MY DELIVERER;
MY GOD IS MY ROCK, IN WHOM I TAKE REFUGE.

PSALM 18:2

"IF ANYONE WOULD COME AFTER ME, HE MUST DENY HIMSELF
AND TAKE UP HIS CROSS AND FOLLOW ME."

MATTHEW 16:24

THE WORD OF THE LORD IS RIGHT AND TRUE;
HE IS FAITHFUL IN ALL HE DOES.

PSALM 33:4

THE LORD IS MY STRENGTH, MY SHIELD FROM EVERY DANGER.
I TRUST IN HIM WITH ALL MY HEART.

PSALM 28:7

IN HIM WE HAVE REDEMPTION THROUGH HIS BLOOD,
THE FORGIVENESS OF SINS, IN ACCORDANCE
WITH THE RICHES OF GOD'S GRACE. EPHESIANS 1:7

I TRUST IN YOUR UNFAILING LOVE. I WILL REJOICE BECAUSE
YOU HAVE RESCUED ME. I WILL SING TO THE LORD BECAUSE
HE HAS BEEN SO GOOD TO ME. PSALM 13:5-6

LIVE A LIFE OF LOVE, JUST AS CHRIST LOVED US AND
GAVE HIMSELF UP FOR US AS A FRAGRANT OFFERING
AND SACRIFICE TO GOD. EPHESIANS 5:2

"YOU WILL CALL UPON ME AND COME AND PRAY TO ME, AND I WILL
LISTEN TO YOU. YOU WILL SEEK ME AND FIND ME WHEN YOU SEEK ME
WITH ALL YOUR HEART." JEREMIAH 29:12-13

MY SOUL FINDS REST IN GOD ALONE; MY SALVATION COMES FROM HIM.

PSALM 62:1

DELIGHT YOURSELF IN THE LORD,
AND HE WILL GIVE YOU THE DESIRES OF YOUR HEART.

PSALM 37:4

THE LORD IS MY LIGHT AND MY SALVATION—
WHOM SHALL I FEAR? THE LORD IS THE STRONGHOLD OF
MY LIFE—OF WHOM SHALL I BE AFRAID? PSALM 27:1

THE LORD HIMSELF GOES BEFORE YOU AND WILL BE WITH YOU;
HE WILL NEVER LEAVE YOU NOR FORSAKE YOU.

DEUTERONOMY 31:8

GOD IS WORKING IN YOU, GIVING YOU THE DESIRE
TO OBEY HIM AND THE POWER TO DO WHAT PLEASES HIM.

PHILIPPIANS 2:13

I CAN DO EVERYTHING THROUGH CHRIST, WHO GIVES ME STRENGTH.

PHILIPPIANS 4:13

IF YOU WANT TO KNOW WHAT GOD WANTS YOU TO DO,
ASK HIM, AND HE WILL GLADLY TELL YOU.

JAMES 1:5

CREATE IN ME A PURE HEART, O GOD,
AND RENEW A STEADFAST SPIRIT WITHIN ME.

PSALM 51:10

IF ANYONE IS IN CHRIST, HE IS A NEW CREATION;
THE OLD HAS GONE, THE NEW HAS COME!

2 CORINTHIANS 5:17

CAST YOUR CARES ON THE LORD AND HE WILL SUSTAIN YOU.

PSALM 55:22

THE LORD YOUR GOD IS WITH YOU, HE IS MIGHTY TO SAVE.
HE WILL TAKE GREAT DELIGHT IN YOU, HE WILL QUIET YOU
WITH HIS LOVE. ZEPHANIAH 3:17

THE LORD IS FAITHFUL TO ALL HIS PROMISES
AND LOVING TOWARD ALL HE HAS MADE.

PSALM 145:13

IN YOU, O LORD, DO I PUT MY TRUST AND CONFIDENTLY
TAKE REFUGE; LET ME NEVER BE PUT TO SHAME OR CONFUSION!

PSALM 71:1

"BE STRONG AND COURAGEOUS . . . THE LORD YOUR GOD
WILL BE WITH YOU WHEREVER YOU GO."

JOSHUA 1:9

DEPEND ON THE LORD IN WHATEVER YOU DO,
AND YOUR PLANS WILL SUCCEED.

PROVERBS 16:3

SINCE WE HAVE BEEN JUSTIFIED THROUGH FAITH,
WE HAVE PEACE WITH GOD THROUGH OUR LORD JESUS CHRIST.

ROMANS 5:1

THE LORD IS MY ROCK, MY FORTRESS AND MY DELIVERER;
MY GOD IS MY ROCK, IN WHOM I TAKE REFUGE.

PSALM 18:2

"IF ANYONE WOULD COME AFTER ME, HE MUST DENY HIMSELF
AND TAKE UP HIS CROSS AND FOLLOW ME."

MATTHEW 16:24

THE WORD OF THE LORD IS RIGHT AND TRUE;
HE IS FAITHFUL IN ALL HE DOES.

PSALM 33:4

THE LORD IS MY STRENGTH, MY SHIELD FROM EVERY DANGER.
I TRUST IN HIM WITH ALL MY HEART.

PSALM 28:7

IN HIM WE HAVE REDEMPTION THROUGH HIS BLOOD,
THE FORGIVENESS OF SINS, IN ACCORDANCE
WITH THE RICHES OF GOD'S GRACE. EPHESIANS 1:7

I TRUST IN YOUR UNFAILING LOVE. I WILL REJOICE BECAUSE
YOU HAVE RESCUED ME. I WILL SING TO THE LORD BECAUSE
HE HAS BEEN SO GOOD TO ME. PSALM 13:5-6

LIVE A LIFE OF LOVE, JUST AS CHRIST LOVED US AND
GAVE HIMSELF UP FOR US AS A FRAGRANT OFFERING
AND SACRIFICE TO GOD. EPHESIANS 5:2

"YOU WILL CALL UPON ME AND COME AND PRAY TO ME, AND I WILL LISTEN TO YOU. YOU WILL SEEK ME AND FIND ME WHEN YOU SEEK ME WITH ALL YOUR HEART." JEREMIAH 29:12-13

MY SOUL FINDS REST IN GOD ALONE; MY SALVATION COMES FROM HIM.

PSALM 62:1